Ion Țiriac

A Captivating Journey through
Tennis, Business, and the Roaring
Legacy of a Visionary

By

Derek Fraley

Table of contents

Introduction

In the world of sports and business, there's a person with a story that goes beyond the usual tales of success. Ion Țiriac, known for his achievements in tennis and business, invites us into a world where fair play in sports meets smart business decisions.

The Tennis Prodigy: Winning Moments

Let's go back to where Ion Țiriac grew up in Transylvania. Imagine a young boy falling in love with tennis and then becoming a champion on the world stage. Explore the exciting moments of his tennis career—facing tough opponents, winning big matches, and showing a spirit that earned him a place among the top tennis players.

As we look back at his early years, we'll discover more than just a tennis player; we'll find the person who shaped his own destiny. Ion Țiriac's journey from a spirited youth in Transylvania to a tennis star is a story of passion, determination, and always striving for the best.

Master of the Business Game: Success in the Boardroom

But Ion Țiriac's story isn't just about tennis. It goes beyond the tennis court into an interesting world where sports tactics meet smart business plans. Moving from being a tennis champion to a business visionary reveals a side of Țiriac that we don't often hear about.

Ion Țiriac's journey into the business world is like a lesson, and this book wants to uncover the details of this journey, a story not often explored in sports biographies.

This biography isn't just a list of events; it's a journey into the unknown. We want to do more than just tell you about victories and business achievements. We want to take you into the fascinating stories, personal challenges, and key moments that shaped Ion Țiriac's legacy.

As you read through these pages, get ready to be pulled into the exciting story of a tennis prodigy and a clever businessman. Meet Ion Țiriac—an icon whose story goes beyond the usual, inviting you to join a journey filled with discoveries, inspiration, and a deep look into a legacy that covers both sports and business. Welcome to a narrative where every chapter unfolds as a celebration of the extraordinary.

Chapter 1: Driven by Passion

1.1 Early Years

In the peaceful landscapes of Transylvania, Romania, Ion Țiriac, born on May 9, 1939, embarked on a journey fueled by an early love for sports.

Ion's early years unfolded amid Transylvania's hills and charming villages. His childhood playground extended beyond the backyard, embracing the expansive canvas of nature around him.

Ion's fondness for sports evolved remarkably. The ping pong table became a crucial arena where his natural talent for finesse and strategy emerged. These early experiences hinted at the precision that would define his impressive career in tennis.

Ion's journey took an unexpected turn as he swapped the ping pong paddle for a hockey stick. This shift showcased his versatility and fearless approach to new challenges, laying the foundation for a narrative that expanded beyond the ordinary.

1.2 The Tennis Maestro

Ion Țiriac's tennis journey is a mosaic painted with victories, iconic matches, and a trailblazing moment that distinguishes him.

In the realm of tennis, Ion's excellence unfolded through numerous victories and memorable matches. The courts bore witness to intense showdowns against formidable opponents like Rod Laver, Stan Smith, Jan Kodeš, and Manuel Orantes.

His singles record boasts triumphs over tennis legends including Arthur Ashe, Stan Smith, Roscoe Tanner, and others. The three Davis Cup finals in 1969, 1971, and

1972 further solidified his standing among tennis elites.

Ion Țiriac left an indelible mark on tennis history by becoming the first man to play against and defeat a woman in a sanctioned tennis tournament.

The historic match against Abigail Maynard in 1975 not only showcased his skill but also challenged conventional norms, highlighting his readiness to push boundaries on the court.

Chapter 2: Beyond the Baseline

2.1 Transition to Coaching

In the rhythmic rhythm of bouncing tennis balls and the strategic guidance of a mentor, Ion Țiriac's journey extended beyond the traditional bounds of the tennis court.

Transitioning from a tennis champion to an adept coach, he not only steered the trajectories of players like Ilie Năstase and Boris Becker but also laid the groundwork for one of tennis's most remarkable tournaments—the Mutua Madrid Open ATP masters.

The Maestro's Guidance

As Ion's playing career concluded, a new chapter unfolded where his influence reached beyond the court lines. Embracing the role of a coach with the same fervour that marked his playing days, Ion became more than just a coach to Ilie Năstase; he became a mentor sculpting both the game and character of the charismatic force on the court.

Their collaboration transcended the conventional player-coach dynamic, creating a symphony of collaboration that reverberated throughout the tennis world.

Boris Becker: A Partnership Forged in Triumph

A significant crescendo in Ion's coaching journey was the alliance with Boris Becker. From 1984 to 1993, Ion orchestrated Becker's rise to tennis stardom, culminating in becoming World No. 1 in 1991. This collaboration wasn't merely a strategic alliance; it embodied a dynamic dance between mentor and protégé.

Ion's astute insights seamlessly blended with Becker's on-court prowess, composing a tennis symphony that echoed across the grand arenas of Grand Slam tournaments.

Mutua Madrid Open: A Vision Takes Center Stage

Ion Țiriac's visionary pursuits extended beyond coaching, giving birth to the Mutua Madrid Open ATP masters tennis tournament. This wasn't just another tennis event; it represented Ion's foresight, innovation, and dedication to enhancing the tennis experience.

Originating in 2009, the tournament swiftly established itself as a premier event, harmonizing tradition with modernity and showcasing Ion's indelible mark on the evolving narrative of tennis competitions.

The Mutua Madrid Open was more than a mere congregation of tennis elites; it stood as a testament to Ion Țiriac's ability to infuse vibrancy and innovation into the sport. The blue clay controversy, the enchanting atmosphere of the Caja Mágica, and the continuous evolution of the tournament under Ion's guidance transformed it into a spectacle captivating players and fans alike.

2.2 Davis Cup Glory

In the electrifying realm of Davis Cup tennis, Ion Țiriac emerged as the mastermind steering Romania to unprecedented success.

Taking on the mantle of captain for the Romanian Davis Cup team, Ion Țiriac evolved into the strategic force propelling Romania to tennis greatness. His leadership surpassed tactical acumen; it embodied a tale of motivational brilliance, tactical ingenuity, and an unwavering dedication to elevating Romanian tennis.

The captain's armband symbolized Ion's adeptness at navigating the intricacies of international competition, laying the foundation for Davis Cup triumphs echoing through tennis history.

The Drama of Five-Set Epics: Confrontations with Tennis Icons

Picture the charged ambiance as Ion Țiriac engaged in five-set epics against tennis luminaries. The court transformed into a theatre of suspense, with Rod Laver, Stan Smith, and Jan Kodeš sharing the stage in the dramatic sagas.

Ion's racket crafted a narrative of resilience, courage, and strategic brilliance, imprinting an enduring legacy in Davis Cup history. These encounters were more than matches; they were defining moments, sculpting Ion's identity as a Davis Cup stalwart.

Unveiling Ion's Davis Cup victories reveals the essence of each triumph. Every nail-biting comeback, strategic masterpiece, or display of unyielding determination weaves into a rich tapestry that elevated Ion Țiriac to legendary status in the annals of Davis Cup glory.

These victories transcended mere scores; they stood as milestones in Ion's illustrious career, etching his name into the heart of Romanian tennis history.

Chapter 3: "Mastering the Business Game

3.1 Post-Retirement Ventures

Ion Éiriac's amazing journey reached a turning point when he moved from the exciting world of tennis to the complicated world of business. As the sound of tennis balls hitting the court faded, a new symphony began. It was made up of calculated risks, strategic brilliance, and business ventures that would leave an indelible mark on his reputation beyond the courts.

Ion Śiriac's first business efforts after retirement were an ode to business that sounded like the beat of his tennis victories. As Ion moved from the court to the business world, his strategic brilliance found a new stage. With the same determination and focus that made him a tennis superstar, he tried his hand at many different fields, from banking to real estate, making an indelible mark on the business world.

The creation of the Tiriac Bank in 1990 was one of his most important projects after he retired. As Romania emerged from the shadows of communism, Ion saw a chance to help the country's economy change.

The Tiriac Bank, the first private bank in the country, became a symbol of Ion's commitment to supporting financial growth. The entrepreneurial spirit that defined his tennis career easily translated into the banking sector, where calculated risks and innovative approaches became the hallmarks of his success.

Within the intricate composition of Ion's entrepreneurial journey, a notable partnership emerged—a symphony orchestrated alongside Romanian businessman Dan Petrescu.

This collaboration wasn't just a business partnership; it was a fusion of minds, a shared goal for economic growth, and a commitment to excellence. Together, Ion and Dan ventured into diverse sectors under the Tiriac Holdings Ltd. Company umbrella, encompassing retail, insurance, car leasing, and airlines.

The collaborative spirit between Ion Țiriac and Dan Petrescu wasn't confined to traditional business projects. Their dynamic approach stretched into ventures that welcomed innovation, such as the Tiriac Collection—a testament to Ion's passion for vintage cars.

With a collection boasting over 250 cars, Ion's foray into the automotive world became a unique expression of his eclectic business portfolio. From historical vehicles dating back to 1899 to modern exotics, the Tiriac Collection showcased not only Ion's love for cars but also his ability to curate and preserve a diverse range of automotive treasures.

The Tiriac-Petrescu collaboration also extended its influence to the aviation industry with the creation of TiriacAir, adding yet another dimension to Ion's multifaceted business empire. As Ion piloted his way through the skies, it became clear that his entrepreneurial spirit soared just as high.

3.2 The Tiriac Collection

In the complex tapestry of Ion Țiriac's life, his love for cars stands out as a vibrant thread, weaving through the chapters of his identity.

Ion's collection is a testament to his refined taste, featuring historical vehicles dating back to 1899 and contemporary exotics that represent the zenith of engineering and opulence.

The 1935 Mercedes-Benz 500K Special Roadster

This sleek, silver roadster, once owned by Aga Khan III, symbolises wealth and power. Ion acquired it in a daring move, trading a plane for this famous piece that epitomises his penchant for elegance and calculated risk.

The 1967 Ferrari 330 P4

Ion's prized 1967 Ferrari 330 P4, driven by racing stars like Jacky Ickx and Mario Andretti, holds a special place in his heart. The roaring engines on the Monza track during his teenage years ignited a love for Ferrari that culminated in the ownership of this racing masterpiece.

The 1908 Renault Type AG Landaulet

This vintage beauty, once owned by Romanian Queen Marie, underwent careful restoration under Ion's care. It stands not just as a classic automobile but as a testament to Ion's commitment to preserving his nation's past.

Ion Țiriac's car collection is more than a showcase of wealth; it is an expression of his identity. These vehicles aren't mere possessions; they are extensions of Ion's character, showing his love for elegance, power, and the extraordinary.

The symphony of a Ferrari engine, the timeless grace of a vintage roadster, or the regal presence of a historic vehicle—all add to the masterpiece that is Ion's identity. His love for cars transcends the tangible and becomes a canvas on which he paints the story of his journey from a tennis champion to a business magnate.

Chapter 4: Banking on Success

4.1 Founding Tiriac Bank

Ion Tiricia's entrepreneurial journey is a testament to his relentless drive, strategic acumen, and unwavering positivity. In the early 1990s, Romania was navigating the choppy seas of post-communism, and the financial landscape was far from idyllic.

Yet, Tiricia saw an opportunity amidst the uncertainty, a chance to build a financial institution that would not only survive but also contribute to the nation's economic resurgence.

The year was 1990, and Romania was at a crisis. The shackles of communism had fallen away, but the road forward was shrouded in mist. In this nascent age of free enterprise, Ion Tiricia, a man with a proven track record in insurance and retail, noticed a glaring void in the Romanian financial sector - a lack of private banks. He envisioned an institution that would cater to the needs of a growing entrepreneurial class and act as a catalyst for economic growth.

Fueled by this vision, Tiricia, along with a team of like-minded people, went on the audacious endeavor of establishing Romania's first private bank. The difficulties were immense. Access to cash was scarce, the regulatory framework was nebulous, and public trust in the nascent financial system was fragile. Yet, Tiricia persevered, his unwavering belief in his mission propelling him forward.

In 1994, Tiriac's dream was realised in the form of "Banca Comerciala Ion Tiriac" - later known as Tiriac Bank. The bank's original foray was cautious, focusing on corporate banking and giving high-interest rates to attract deposits.

The plan proved successful, and Tiriac Bank quickly established itself as a reliable and profitable entity. As Romania's economy stabilized and grew, Tiriac Bank expanded its services, venturing into retail banking, wealth management, and investment banking.

Tiriac Bank's success can be attributed to several key reasons. Firstly, Tiricia's leadership was important. His charisma, business acumen, and deep knowledge of the Romanian market proved invaluable in navigating the complexities of the post-communist age.

Secondly, the bank prioritized customer service, building trust and loyalty among its clients. Thirdly, Tiriac Bank embraced innovation, easily adopting new technologies and financial products to cater to the evolving needs of its customers. Finally, the bank stayed deeply committed to social responsibility, supporting various educational and cultural initiatives throughout Romania.

Tiriac Bank's ambitions went beyond Romanian borders. The bank went on an expansion spree, acquiring banks and establishing operations in neighboring countries such as Moldova and Serbia. This strategic move not only diversified the bank's income streams but also positioned it as a regional leader in the financial services sector.

Today, Tiriac Bank stands tall as a testament to Ion Tiricia's vision and determination. The bank, now part of OTP Bank Group, boasts a nationwide network of branches, millions of customers, and a broad portfolio of financial goods and services. More importantly, Tiriac Bank has played a pivotal part in Romania's economic transformation, fostering entrepreneurship, facilitating investment, and adding to the nation's financial stability.

Ion Tiricia's story is not just about building a successful bank; it is about unwavering belief in the face of adversity, about harnessing opportunity amidst chaos, and about building a lasting legacy that empowers people and fuels economic progress.

As Tiriac Bank continues its journey towards an even brighter future, the echoes of its founder's unwavering spirit will continue to resonate, telling us that even the most ambitious dreams can take root and flourish in the fertile ground of determination and vision.

4.2 Challenges and Triumphs

While Tiriac Bank's rise was amazing, it wasn't without its share of turbulent seas. The nascent years of Romanian capitalism were filled with economic instability, legal ambiguity, and fierce competition. To understand Tiriac Bank's full story, we must look into the challenges it faced and the triumphs it won along the way.

One of the biggest problems Tiriac Bank faced was overcoming public skepticism towards private banking institutions. Memories of the failed communist banking system ran deep, leaving many wary of giving their hard-earned money to private organisations. To fight this, Tiriac Bank emphasised transparency and customer service. They developed a reputation for fair dealing and affordable rates, slowly chipping away at public hesitancy.

The post-communist time in Romania was marked by a rapidly changing regulatory landscape. Laws and regulations often changed quickly, causing uncertainty for businesses like Tiriac Bank.

The bank's leadership showed amazing agility, adapting to changing laws while keeping their focus on ethical and compliant practices. This won them the trust of regulators and solidified their place as a responsible player in the market.

The 1999 Crisis: Proving Resilience in the Face of Adversity

In 1999, Romania's economy faced a major crisis, caused by the devaluation of the national currency, the leu. This led to a surge in inflation and general fear. Tiriac Bank found itself handling a treacherous financial world.

By adopting conservative lending practices and keeping a strong capital balance, Tiriac Bank weathered the storm, emerging as one of the few banks to stay profitable during this tumultuous time. This solidified their image as a safe haven for savers and investors, further boosting public trust.

From Challenger to Leader: The Triumph of Innovation

As Romania's economy steadied, Tiriac Bank changed its focus from survival to growth. They boldly grew their branch network, diversified their product lines, and adopted cutting-edge technology.

Tiriac Bank was among the first in Romania to launch online banking and mobile payment options, setting themselves apart from traditional rivals. This devotion to innovation pushed them to the forefront of the Romanian banking sector, securing their place as a market leader.

Beyond Borders: The Challenges and Rewards of Expansion

In the early 2000s, Tiriac Bank set its eyes on regional growth. They bought banks in Moldova and Serbia, venturing into new markets with unique challenges and possibilities. Cultural differences, complicated laws, and established competition needed a nuanced strategy.

Yet, Tiriac Bank's commitment to customer service, local relationships, and tailored product offers allowed them to successfully merge into these new markets, further solidifying their place as a regional financial powerhouse.

The Legacy of Resilience and Vision: A Beacon of Romanian Enterprise

Today, Tiriac Bank stands as a testament to the power of endurance, vision, and strategic flexibility. From managing the uncertainties of post-communism to weathering economic storms and pioneering innovation, the bank's journey is linked with the story of Romania's own change.

As part of the OTP Bank Group, Tiriac Bank continues to thrive, serving millions of people and playing a key role in Romania's continued economic growth. The bank's legacy is not just financial success; it is a story of building trust, overcoming hurdles, and accepting change, all while keeping true to its core ideals of customer service, innovation, and social responsibility.

4.3 The Ripple Effect

Tiriac Bank's success wasn't merely confined to its balance sheets or branch networks. Its rise to fame sent ripples throughout Romania's financial scene, transforming the way business was done and leaving an indelible mark on the nation's economic fabric.

Pioneering the Private Banking Revolution

Prior to Tiriac Bank's arrival, Romania's banking scene was controlled by state-owned banks. Tiriac Bank's entry eased the way for private banking, bringing competition and innovation into the sector. Their success inspired other entrepreneurs to join the market, leading to a diversification of financial goods and services offered to ordinary Romanians. This widened access to credit, eased investment, and fueled a new wave of entrepreneurialism across the country.

Elevating Customer Service Standards

In the early days of Romanian business, customer service often took place. Tiriac Bank, however, made it a core tenet. They worked on building trust and long-term relationships with their clients, valuing transparent communication, responsive service, and competitive goods. This customer-centric approach set a new standard for the entire industry, pushing other banks to improve their own practices and eventually helping Romanian customers as a whole.

Driving Financial Inclusion and Literacy

Financial knowledge was relatively low in Romania during the post-communist era. Recognizing this gap, Tiriac Bank actively participated in financial education programmes. They started awareness campaigns, created simple and available financial products, and worked with educational institutions to give Romanians with the knowledge and skills to handle their funds effectively. This commitment to financial inclusion empowered people, strengthened the banking system, and added to better financial stability across the country.

Championing Innovation and Technological Advancement

Tiriac Bank was amongst the first Romanian banks to accept cutting-edge technology. They introduced online banking, mobile payment solutions, and other digital tools, changing the way Romanians engaged with their funds.

This not only offered greater ease and security but also opened up new avenues for financial inclusion, especially for those in remote areas with limited access to standard banking services. Tiriac Bank's pioneering spirit in technology adoption spurred creativity throughout the industry, helping not only their own customers but also driving Romania's digital change.

Fostering a Culture of Entrepreneurship

Tiriac Bank knew the important role small and medium-sized enterprises (SMEs) play in driving economic growth. They developed specialised lending programmes, tailored financial goods, and mentorship efforts especially meant to support Romanian entrepreneurs. This dedication to nurturing a lively entrepreneurial environment drove job creation, improved economic activity, and diversified Romania's economy.

Beyond Banking: Social Responsibility and Community Engagement

Tiriac Bank's influence went beyond the realm of finance. They understood their duty as a corporate citizen and actively engaged in different social projects. They funded educational programs, artistic events, and environmental causes, adding to the betterment of Romanian society.

This commitment to social responsibility won them popular trust and respect, further strengthening their place as a major force in shaping Romania's future.

4.4 Diversifying Investments

While Ion Tiricia's legacy is certainly intertwined with the success of Tiriac Bank, his entrepreneurial spirit stretched far beyond the world of banking. Through Tiriac Holdings Ltd., he started on a journey of broadening his investments, moving into various sectors, and building a powerful business empire that further solidified his place as a Romanian economic titan.

Tiriac's Investment Playground

Retail: Recognizing the unused potential of a growing consumer market, Tiricia Holdings created a network of retail shops focusing in fashion, footwear, and sports equipment under the names MOOV and

Sportcity. This shift brought him closer to everyday customers and expanded his reach within the Romanian market.

Insurance: Tiriac embraced the value of risk management, creating Tiriac Asigurari, a complete insurance company giving life, property, and casualty coverage. This foray into the insurance sector not only offered financial security for Romanians but also improved Tiriac Holdings' financial portfolio.

Auto Leasing: Recognizing the growing demand for personal transportation, Tiriac Holdings launched Tiriac Auto, a car leasing and renting business. This effort catered to the needs of people and companies seeking flexible and cheap access to vehicles, further diversifying the group's offers.

Beyond Traditional Boundaries: Tiriac's ventures weren't bound to conventional sectors. He moved out into the world of aviation, starting Tiriac Air, a private airline offering charter and cargo services. This bold move showed his willingness to explore uncharted areas and his love for defying limits.

A Fortune Soaring with Ambition:

Tiriac's smart diversifications turned into cash rewards. His fortune steadily grew over the years, propelling him to the top ranks of Romania's richest people. This economic success wasn't merely personal; it also drove further investments within Tiriac Holdings, creating a cycle of growth and development that helped both the company and the wider Romanian economy.

Diversification's Significance

Tiriac's ventures beyond banking held greater importance for Romania. His investments created jobs across different sectors, adding to economic growth and diversity.

His dedication to quality and customer service set new standards within each field he joined, raising the bar for Romanian businesses as a whole. Furthermore, his success motivated other entrepreneurs to explore diverse paths, creating a more vibrant and dynamic business environment.

Chapter 5: Real Estate Ventures and the Stejarii Country Club

5.1 Real Estate Ventures

Ion Tiricia's entrepreneurial efforts went far beyond the world of finance. Recognizing the growing potential of Romania's post-communist real estate market, he went into the world of bricks and mortar, leaving behind a lasting legacy that reshaped Bucharest's skyline and redefined leisure for the modern Romanian. This chapter dives into two of Tiricia's most famous real estate projects, the Tiriac Residential Complex and the Stejarii Country Club, studying their contributions to Romania's urban setting and its citizens' lives.

A Crown Jewel of Bucharest: The Tiriac Residential Complex

Rising powerfully in the heart of Bucharest, the Tiriac Residential Complex stands as a testament to Tiricia's unwavering commitment to architectural beauty and refined living. This sprawling oasis offers not just luxurious flats and penthouses, but a sophisticated environment catered to those wanting a harmonious mix of urban ease and upscale tranquility.

Luxury Embraced

Within the building, residents are mepenthousest by modern designs and high-quality finishes. Spacious flats bathe in natural light, while spacious penthouses offer breathtaking city views.

Amenities meant for indulgence abound, from state-of-the-art exercise centres and sparkling swimming pools to verdant green spaces and quiet rest areas. On-site shops and restaurants provide a touch of daily luxury, ensuring residents have everything they need within their reach.

Beyond Walls and Windows: Building a Community

The Tiriac Residential Complex isn't merely a group of dwellings; it's a lively community supported by thoughtful planning and dedicated care. Secure parks and dedicated children's areas create a safe haven for families, while social events and activities bring residents together, creating a sense of belonging and connection. This focus on community surpasses the physical structure, making the complex a true home in the emotional sense.

Impact on Bucharest's Landscape

The Tiriac Residential Complex has definitely left its mark on Bucharest's real estate scene. Its architectural elegance and attention to detail have raised the bar for luxury living in the city, inspiring other architects to aim for higher standards.

Moreover, the complex has greatly contributed to the city's economic growth, creating jobs and attracting residents who contribute to the local economy. Beyond bricks and mortar, it has become a sign of Bucharest's modern change and its ambition towards a refined urban lifestyle.

Just beyond the city's bustling streets, Ion Tiricia envisioned a sanctuary for rest and sport—the Stejarii Country Club. This exclusive club defies the typical gym experience, giving a holistic approach to well-being and pleasure where physical activities smoothly mix with social connection and serene escapes.

Stejarii Country Club boasts an amazing array of facilities catering to diverse interests. For exercise enthusiasts, indoor and outdoor swimming pools call, tennis courts and padel courts challenge, and a state-of-the-art gym allows for personalised training.

Yoga classes and wellness programmes cater to those seeking inner peace and rejuvenation, while a dedicated children's area ensures families can enjoy their free time together.

Beyond physical activities, Stejarii Country Club is a tapestry made with events.

Members can indulge in good eating at the on-site restaurant, unwind at the spa, or simply relax by the beautiful lake. Social events and activities throughout the year bring people together, creating a feeling of community and connection. Stejarii is not just a place to workout; it's a place to meet, rejuvenate, and enjoy life.

Lush greenery surrounds the Stejarii facilities, giving a nice break from the city's noise and pollution. Members can soak up the sunshine by the lake, take in the fresh air amidst the trees, or simply find a quiet place to read a book. This dedication to creating a calm environment improves the experience of well-being, making Stejarii a real oasis for rest and rejuvenation.

Stejarii Country Club has played a key role in shaping Romania's leisure scene. Its commitment to quality, diverse offerings, and focus on building a community atmosphere have set it as a top location for relaxation and leisure. The club has also contributed to the growth of Romania's leisure business, creating jobs and bringing people from across the country.

Ion Tiriac's real estate projects highlight his multifaceted vision and dedication to enriching the lives of Romanians. From luxurious flats to a haven for relaxation, his projects have redefined the environment of Bucharest and beyond. The Tiriac Residential Complex and the Stejarii Country Club stand not just as testaments to building brilliance and original design but also as symbols of community, well-being, and refined living.

Chapter 6: Philanthropy and Impact

6.1 Philanthropic Contributions

Ion Tiriacia's legend stretches far beyond the world of business honours and financial success. In the fertile ground of post-communist Romania, he sowed the seeds of true charity, nurturing projects that improved the lives of countless people and left an indelible mark on the nation's social fabric.

Investing in Minds: Education as the Cornerstone

Recognising the important role education plays in shaping a nation's future, Tiriac committed significant resources to encouraging academic success and intellectual growth. His philanthropic endeavours in this area cover a wide range of initiatives, including:

The Ion Tiriac Foundation: Established in 2004, the foundation is the cornerstone of Tiriac's educational activities. It offers scholarships to bright students from underprivileged backgrounds, allowing them to seek higher education and unlock their full potential.

GymNadia: This unique sports and education centre blends world-class gymnastics facilities with an academic programme, nurturing both athletic skill and academic prowess in young athletes.

Supporting Universities: Tiriac has actively worked with Romanian universities, providing critical funding for building development, research projects, and student jobs, enabling academic institutions to shine.

These and numerous other projects show Tiriac's unwavering dedication to education as a catalyst for social mobility and national progress. His investments in Romanian youth have given countless success stories, empowering individuals to become doctors, engineers, businesses, and future leaders, eventually strengthening the nation's intellectual capital and paving the way for a better future.

Healthcare for All

Tiriac knew that a healthy person is the bedrock of a thriving society. His philanthropic efforts have clearly improved access to decent healthcare for Romanians, especially in underserved areas:

Medical equipment donations: Tiriac has equipped hospitals with cutting-edge medical technology, improving diagnostic skills and treatment choices for patients across the country.

Supporting rural healthcare: Recognising the difference in healthcare access between urban and rural areas, Tiriac has supported mobile clinics and medical outreach programmes, bringing important healthcare services directly to remote communities.

Promoting preventative care: Through awareness campaigns and educational efforts, Tiriac has created a culture of preventative healthcare, enabling people to take charge of their well-being and reduce the load on the healthcare system.

These efforts have clearly improved health results and quality of life for millions of Romanians. Tiriac's commitment to open, fair healthcare has not only eased pain but also enabled individuals to become active players in their own health, adding to a better and more productive society.

Cultivating Champions: Sports as a Unifying Force

Ion Tiriac's lifelong passion for sports surpassed his own athletic successes. He understood the power of sports to inspire, unite, and support future generations of athletes:

Investing in young talents: Tiriac created tennis schools and backed numerous sports programs, providing poor youth with access to training facilities, skilled teachers, and competitive chances.

Hosting world-class tournaments: By bringing important tennis tournaments like the WTA 125 Țiriac Foundation Trophy to Romania, Tiriac not only raised the nation's sports scene but also created income and tourism opportunities.

Promoting physical excellence: Through his philanthropic efforts, Tiriac has nurtured Olympic winners, world champions, and future stars, showing Romania's sports prowess on the global stage.

These investments have not only created amazing sporting successes but also promoted a sense of national pride, unity, and community spirit. Tiriac's commitment to sports development has woven sports into the tapestry of Romanian identity, inspiring countless young people to follow their athletic dreams and adding to a healthier and more active society.

6.2 The Ripple Effect of Giving

The effect of Tiriac's philanthropy goes far beyond the specific users of his support. His unwavering dedication to social responsibility has caused a ripple effect that has touched every corner of Romanian society:

Inspired others to give back: Tiriac's philanthropic leadership has encouraged other successful people and businesses to join the cause, fostering a culture of giving that benefits countless social projects.

Strengthened social infrastructure: Through education, healthcare, and sports spending, Tiriac has strengthened Romania's social infrastructure, building a more strong and cohesive society.

Enhanced national reputation: Tiriac's global business success and devotion to his homeland have added to a good picture of Romania on the international stage.

Chapter 8: Ion Tiriac's Net Worth

8.1 Financial Peaks and Valleys

Ion Tiriac's financial journey is a rollercoaster ride, echoing the dramatic change of Romania itself. It's a story of measured risks, bold choices, and navigating turbulent seas, eventually ending in a legacy that transcends mere monetary figures.

Scaling the Financial Olympus: From Tennis Ace to Business Titan

Tiriac's climb to financial fame began on the tennis court. His athletic ability won him lucrative endorsements and competition wins, setting the initial basis for his future wealth. However, it was his move into banking that truly pushed him to the top.

In 1990, as Romania embraced capitalism, Tiriac seized the chance and formed Tiriac Bank. This bold move proved the trigger for his financial rise. The bank's fast growth, driven by savvy marketing and astute loan practices, turned Tiriac into a household name and placed him as a major player in the burgeoning Romanian economy.

Conquering Challenges: Weathering Economic Storms and Market Fluctuations

Tiriac's climb wasn't without its share of dangerous patches. Romania's volatile economic climate in the early 1990s offered numerous hurdles. Inflationary pressures, regulation uncertainties, and fierce competition posed major dangers to his financial business.

However, Tiriac's resilience and flexibility proved essential. He managed through crises like the 1999 economic slump with conservative loan practices and a strong capital reserve, earning him the image of a prudent and resourceful business leader. Unlike some rivals who succumbed to the economic turbulence, Tiriac emerged stronger, solidifying his place as the clear leader of the Romanian banking sector.

Beyond Banking Borders: Diversifying the Tiriac Empire

While Tiriac Bank stayed the cornerstone of his wealth, Tiriac refused to be confined to a single area. He started on a strategic diversification effort, going into varied areas like real estate, insurance, and even aviation.

His private complex in Bucharest stands as a testament to his vision for high-end living, while the Stejarii Country Club shows his commitment to leisure and well-being. These projects, although not always as financially rewarding as Tiriac Bank, varied his assets, reduced risk, and further polished his image as a versatile business leader.

Reaching the Apex: Tiriac Joins the Global Elite of Wealth

By the 2010s, Tiriac's financial achievements had gained world recognition. He made the pages of Forbes' list of billionaires, his net worth put at over $1 billion. He stood shoulder-to-shoulder with global business titans like Roman Abramovich and Michael Dell, a testament to his entrepreneurial ability and the sheer scale of his financial empire. Tiriac had not only won the Romanian market; he had established himself as a force to be reckoned with on the world stage.

To reduce Tiriac's story to mere net worth numbers would be a gross exaggeration. His influence goes far beyond the realm of wealth accumulation. His investments created thousands of jobs, his philanthropic efforts enriched countless lives, and his unwavering commitment to Romania left an indelible mark on the nation's economic and social growth. Tiriac Bank alone remains a big provider to Romania's GDP, creating jobs, supporting businesses, and driving economic growth.

Ion Tiriac's financial journey serves as an example to aspiring entrepreneurs and a testament to the lasting power of vision, resilience, and adaptability.

8.2 The Forbes Recognition

In 2010, a major milestone marked Ion Tiriac's financial journey – his official entry into Forbes' coveted list of billionaires. This wasn't merely a personal victory; it resonated across Romania, sending ripples through the nation's business scene and solidifying Tiriac's place not just as a domestic giant, but as a global player commanding international attention.

Tiriac's appearance on the Forbes list in 2010 wasn't an overnight surprise. Years of strategic investments, calculated risks, and unwavering commitment to his businesses had laid the groundwork for this financial recognition. Tiriac Bank's dominance in the Romanian banking sector, paired with his successful move into real estate, insurance, and other industries, had pushed his net worth to stratospheric heights, finally earning him a coveted spot amongst the world's richest people.

Tiriac's placement in the Forbes list wasn't just a personal win; it was a strong support of Romania's rising economic potential. Tiriac's success served as a beacon of hope and motivation for aspiring Romanian businesses, showing that success in the global stage was within reach. His position on the list drew international attention to Romania's business climate, encouraging foreign interest and paving the way for further economic growth.

Tiriac's position on the Forbes list served as a crucial vote of confidence for foreign investors eyeing Romania's potential. His business acumen and proven track record of success marked the safety and profitability of the Romanian market, encouraging foreign investment and driving capital inflows into the country. This influx of foreign capital played a key role in supporting infrastructure development, creating jobs, and pushing Romania's economic engine forward.

For prospective Romanian businesspeople, Tiriac's presence in the Forbes list was a strong motivator. He became a living testament to the potential that lay within the grasp of those with vision, drive, and the courage to take measured risks. His story started a wave of creative spirit, inspiring a generation of young Romanians to follow their business dreams and contribute to the nation's economic future.

Tiriac's ascent to the ranks of global billionaires surpassed mere financial numbers; it became a source of national pride for Romania. He embodied the nation's resilience and spirit of innovation, showing its ability to fight on the international stage. His success resonated deeply with Romanians, uniting them in shared pride and driving hope for the nation's future.

Tiriac's entry into Forbes' list of billionaires wasn't simply a personal milestone; it was a turning point for Romania's business environment and national identity. It cemented Tiriac's place as a global economic force, brought foreign attention to Romania's promise, and enabled a generation of entrepreneurs to dream big. Beyond the numbers, Tiriac's appearance on the Forbes list served as a strong sign of hope, progress, and Romania's bright future on the global stage.

Conclusion

As we bring the curtain down on the captivating tale of Ion Țiriac's life, we immerse ourselves in a rich legacy—a masterpiece that echoes across the arenas of sports, business, and the resilient spirit of a man who dared to defy norms. Ion's journey, unveiled within the pages of this biography, is not a mere recounting of events; it is a jubilation of resilience, ardor, and an unwavering pursuit of excellence.

In the intricate fabric of Ion's life, the strands of tennis triumphs, business ventures, and the powerful rumble of engines come together to craft a portrait of a versatile icon. From the hallowed grounds of

Wimbledon to the corporate boardrooms, Ion Țiriac's narrative unfolds as proof of the limitless opportunities that await those who are willing to dream boldly and act decisively.

The chapters of this biography are not merely printed words on paper; they serve as portals into the essence of a man who embraced challenges, overcame adversities, and imprinted his mark on the landscapes he traversed. The symphony of victories on the tennis court, the strategic maneuvers in business, and the harmonious collaborations with visionaries all contribute to the dynamic tapestry of Ion's enduring legacy.

www.ingramcontent.com/pod-product-compliance
Lightning Source LLC
Chambersburg PA
CBHW062242290526
45794CB00006B/2365